MURDER ON THE ORIENT EXPRESS

by
Agatha Christie

Student Packet

Written by
James H. Duncan

Contains masters for:

2	Prereading Activities
7	Vocabulary Activities
1	Study Guide
3	Character Analysis Activities
3	Literary Analysis Activities
2	Comprehension Activities
7	Quizzes
1	Novel Test

PLUS Detailed Answer Key
and Scoring Rubric

Teacher Note

Selected activities, quizzes, and test questions in this Novel Units® Student Packet are labeled with the appropriate reading/language arts skills for quick reference. These skills can be found above quiz/test questions or sections and in the activity headings.

Note

The 2004 Berkley Book edition of the novel, © 1934 by Agatha Christie Limited, was used to prepare this guide. Page references may differ in other editions. Novel ISBN: 978-0-425-20045-2

Please note: Parts of this novel deal with sensitive, mature issues. Please assess the appropriateness of this book for the age level and maturity of your students prior to reading and discussing it with them.

ISBN 978-1-56137-565-3

To order, contact your local school supply store, or—

Novel Units, Inc.
P.O. Box 97
Bulverde, TX 78163-0097

Web site: novelunits.com

Note to the Teacher

Selected activities, quizzes, and test questions in this Novel Units® Student Packet are labeled with the following reading/language arts skills for quick reference. These skills can be found above quiz/test questions or sections and in the activity headings.

Basic Understanding: The student will demonstrate a basic understanding of written texts. The student will:
- use a text's structure or other sources to locate and recall information (Locate Information)
- determine main idea and identify relevant facts and details (Main Idea and Details)
- use prior knowledge and experience to comprehend and bring meaning to a text (Prior Knowledge)
- summarize major ideas in a text (Summarize Major Ideas)

Literary Elements: The student will apply knowledge of literary elements to understand written texts. The student will:
- analyze characters from a story (Character Analysis)
- analyze conflict and problem resolution (Conflict/Resolution)
- recognize and interpret literary devices (flashback, foreshadowing, symbolism, simile, metaphor, etc.) (Literary Devices)
- consider characters' points of view (Point of View)
- recognize and analyze a story's setting (Setting)
- understand and explain themes in a text (Theme)

Analyze Written Texts: The student will use a variety of strategies to analyze written texts. The student will:
- identify the author's purpose (Author's Purpose)
- identify cause and effect relationships in a text (Cause/Effect)
- identify characteristics representative of a given genre (Genre)
- interpret information given in a text (Interpret Text)
- make and verify predictions with information from a text (Predictions)
- sequence events in chronological order (Sequencing)
- identify and use multiple text formats (Text Format)
- follow written directions and write directions for others to follow (Follow/Write Directions)

Critical Thinking: The student will apply critical-thinking skills to analyze written texts. The student will:
- write and complete analogies (Analogies)
- find similarities and differences throughout a text (Compare/Contrast)
- draw conclusions from information given (Drawing Conclusions)
- make and explain inferences (Inferences)
- respond to texts by making connections and observations (Making Connections)
- recognize and identify the mood of a text (Mood)
- recognize an author's style and how it affects a text (Style)
- support responses by referring to relevant aspects of a text (Support Responses)
- recognize and identify the author's tone (Tone)
- write to entertain, such as through humorous poetry or short stories (Write to Entertain)
- write to express ideas (Write to Express)
- write to inform (Write to Inform)
- write to persuade (Write to Persuade)
- demonstrate understanding by creating visual images based on text descriptions (Visualizing)
- practice math skills as they relate to a text (Math Skills)

Name _____

Clue Search

Directions: Collect information about the novel for each of the items. Write down the information, and then make some predictions about the novel.

Information Source	Information Provided
Dedication	
Title	
Cover Illustration	
Teasers on the cover	
Friends' recommendations	
Reviewers' recommendations/awards won	

Your predictions about the novel:

Name _____

Anticipation Guide

Directions: Rate each of the following statements before you read the novel, and discuss your ratings with a partner. After you have completed the novel, rate and discuss the statements again.

1 ——— 2 ——— 3 ——— 4 ——— 5 ——— 6
strongly agree   strongly disagree

	Before	After
1. It is better to be initially suspicious of a stranger than to trust him/her.	_____	_____
2. If the obvious facts suggest that something is impossible, then it probably is.	_____	_____
3. There is no such thing as coincidence.	_____	_____
4. Everyone tells lies from time to time, even honest people.	_____	_____
5. Once someone admits a lie, it is okay to assume that person will be honest from then on.	_____	_____
6. Loyalty is more important than honesty.	_____	_____
7. Anyone who commits a crime must be punished, no matter what.	_____	_____
8. Using stereotypes can help solve a crime.	_____	_____
9. It is easy to solve a crime if all the suspects remain in the same place.	_____	_____
10. People of different nationalities and classes rarely trust each other.	_____	_____

Vocabulary Sentence Sets

resplendent	surreptitious	altercations	peremptory
tyrannical	malevolence	munificent	swarthy
autocratic	demurred	coquetry	slipshod

Directions: Write the vocabulary words on the numbered lines below.

1. _____ 2. _____

3. _____ 4. _____

5. _____ 6. _____

7. _____ 8. _____

9. _____ 10. _____

11. _____ 12. _____

On a separate sheet of paper, use each of the following sets of words in an original sentence. Your sentences should show that you know the meanings of the vocabulary words as they are used in the story.

Sentence 1: words 12 and 4
Sentence 2: words 9 and 3
Sentence 3: words 10 and 2
Sentence 4: words 1 and 7
Sentence 5: words 5 and 2
Sentence 6: words 6 and 3
Sentence 7: words 12 and 11
Sentence 8: words 5 and 6
Sentence 9: words 7 and 9
Sentence 10: words 10 and 8

Vocabulary Definitions

deferential	voluble	kimono	calamity
sardonic	antecedents	memoranda	vexatious
elucidation	imperative	intricacies	redolent

Directions: Choose the word or phrase closest in meaning to the vocabulary word as it is used in the novel. Then, on a separate sheet of paper, use at least four of the vocabulary words in a brief analysis of one character from *Murder on the Orient Express*.

1. **deferential** (a) regrettable (b) reliable (c) respectful (d) refusal

2. **voluble** (a) terrorizing (b) testament (c) temperature (d) talkative

3. **kimono** (a) rime (b) robe (c) ritual (d) rag

4. **calamity** (a) mystery (b) mishap (c) mistake (d) miserly

5. **sardonic** (a) snooty (b) surreal (c) saddened (d) scathing

6. **antecedents** (a) behaviors (b) basics (c) backgrounds (d) benchmarks

7. **memoranda** (a) cables (b) conductions (c) capers (d) communications

8. **vexatious** (a) bothersome (b) brutal (c) brusque (d) bereaved

9. **elucidation** (a) education (b) elation (c) evaporation (d) explanation

10. **imperative** (a) vocal (b) vital (c) vicious (d) vehement

11. **intricacies** (a) dependants (b) details (c) difficulties (d) deviations

12. **redolent** (a) reminiscent (b) resurgent (c) restrictive (d) redundant

Word Map

negligence	gratified	inordinate	draught
pacify	articulate	matron	invalid
aboveboard	enamoured*		

*British spelling used in text

Directions: Complete the word map below for six of the vocabulary words above.

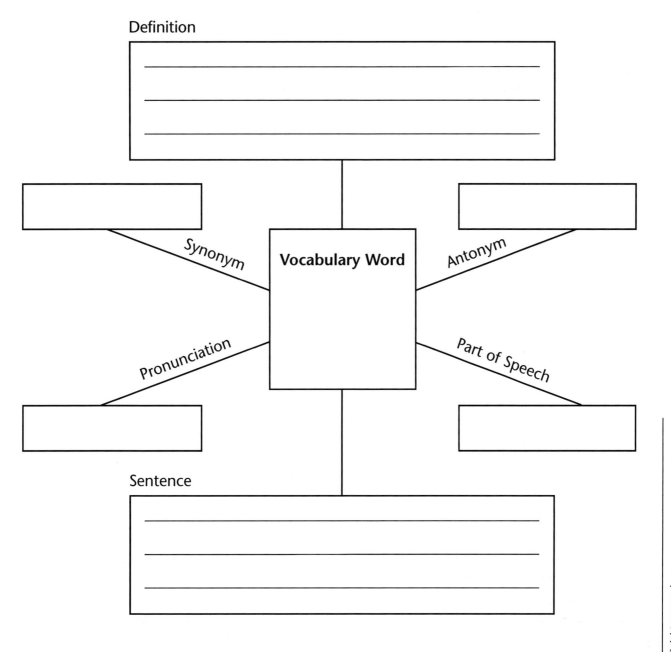

Definition

Synonym

Vocabulary Word

Antonym

Pronunciation

Part of Speech

Sentence

Vocabulary by Association

trional	grudgingly	ascertained	jackanapes
abash	furtive	reverie	sojourn
animus	contemptuous	abominable	impertinent

Directions: Define and associate each vocabulary word above with a character from *Murder on the Orient Express*. In the chart below, explain why that word matches your chosen character. You may associate more than one word with a character, but use no more than two words per character.

Word(s)	Character	Explanation

Synonyms/Antonyms

sang-froid	corroborating	reprovingly	teetotaller
rotundity	embossed	coquettish	truculent
portmanteau	acquiesced	rueful	bequest

Directions: Each sentence below contains an antonym or synonym of a vocabulary word in the box above. Write the related vocabulary word in the provided space, and circle all antonyms.

1. Though she was a light drinker, she enjoyed a glass of wine with her dinner.

   _____

2. The police sought out validating witnesses to support their theory.

   _____

3. Samuel did not care about his inheritance; he missed his grandfather.

   _____

4. No matter how he tried, Jackson could not fit his valise in the trunk of his car.

   _____

5. Michael tried to make his date laugh, but her solemn stare tempered his antics.

   _____

6. The bride was not sure if her dress properly accentuated the slenderness of her arms.

   _____

7. The store manager critically announced each of his employees' faults in public.

   _____

8. Her poise under fire impressed the soldiers, and they no longer questioned her judgment.

   _____

9. The band resisted every change the record company wanted to make to their album.

   _____

10. The boy's defiant attitude did not help the already frustrating situation.

    _____

11. The imprinted design on the novel's cover impressed the writer's fans.

    _____

12. She was unapologetic about her efforts to protect her children.

    _____

Name _____

A Special Sleuth

idiomatic	substantiated	naturalised*	masquerading
didactically	attaché	loquacious	incisive
gainsay	extenuating	indomitable	

*British spelling used in text

Directions: Imagine all the skills and talents it takes to be a good detective, and then create a unique private investigator. On the lines below, describe your one-of-a-kind detective using at least seven of the vocabulary words above.

_____

_____

_____

_____

_____

_____

_____

_____

_____

_____

_____

_____

_____

_____

_____

_____

_____

_____

_____

_____

_____

_____

_____

Crossword Puzzle

preoccupations	geniality	vehemence	inarticulate
enumerated	decorum	exigencies	mosaic
unassailable	earnestness		

Directions: Create a crossword puzzle answer key by filling in the grid below. Be sure to number the squares for each word. Blacken any spaces not used by the letters. Then, write clues to the crossword puzzle. Number the clues to match the numbers in the squares. The teacher will give each student a blank grid. Make a blank copy of your crossword puzzle for other students to answer. Exchange your clues with someone else, and solve the blank puzzle s/he gives you. Check the completed puzzles with the answer keys.

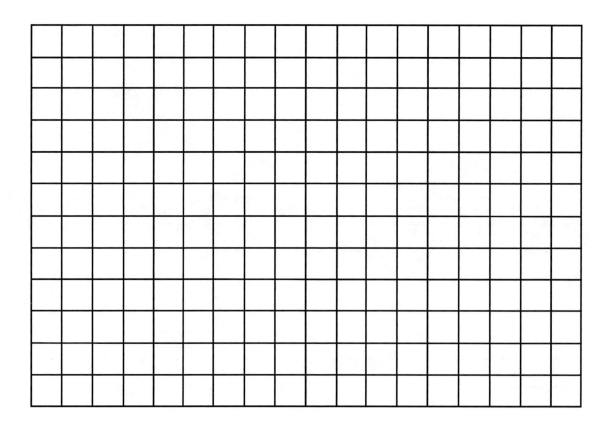

Name _____

Directions: On a separate sheet of paper, write a brief answer to each question as you read the novel at home or in class. Use the questions to guide your reading, prepare for class discussions, and review for quizzes and tests.

Part 1: Chapters 1–4

1. What is Hercule Poirot's first impression of Mary Debenham?

2. How does Mary Debenham react when the train is delayed?

3. What is Poirot's first impression of Ratchett?

4. What curious situation aboard the train does M. Bouc reflect upon with Poirot, and how does Poirot respond?

5. How does M. Bouc describe Princess Dragomiroff?

6. Why is Ratchett worried, and how does Poirot react to Ratchett's offer?

7. What does Mrs. Hubbard tell Poirot about Ratchett?

8. What does Poirot see and hear when a cry wakes him from his sleep?

Part 1: Chapters 5–8

1. What does Poirot learn from the conductor who brings him water?

2. Why has the train stopped? What strange detail does Poirot notice about Mary Debenham?

3. What information does Dr. Constantine provide about Ratchett's death?

4. How does the *chef de train* react to Ratchett's death?

5. In what capacity did MacQueen serve Ratchett?

6. What interesting fact does Poirot notice about the threatening letters?

7. What do Poirot and Dr. Constantine find so strange about the wounds?

8. What piece of evidence is Poirot able to glean from the burnt letter? What is Ratchett's real name?

9. How did the Armstrong family fall apart, and what happened to each member?

10. How does Poirot plan to proceed with his investigation?

Part 2: Chapters 1–6

1. How does M. Bouc describe Pierre Michel?

2. How is MacQueen related to the Armstrong case? How does he feel about Cassetti?

3. What is MacQueen's alibi, and whom did he see walking down the hallway?

4. How are Masterman and Ratchett connected? What is Masterman's alibi?

5. What declaration does Mrs. Hubbard make regarding her experience the night of the murder?

6. What did Mrs. Hubbard have the conductor do when he arrived the night of the murder?

7. Who originally locked Mrs. Hubbard's door?

8. Whose room did Greta Ohlsson enter by mistake, and what happened in those brief moments?

9. What conclusion does M. Bouc settle upon? What does Poirot think of this conclusion?

10. What does Princess Dragomiroff tell Poirot about the Armstrong family?

Part 2: Chapters 7–11

1. How does Count Andrenyi react when Poirot asks to speak to his wife?

2. What is Countess Andrenyi's alibi?

3. Why is Colonel Arbuthnot traveling on the train?

4. What does Colonel Arbuthnot say about the woman in the scarlet kimono?

5. What did Colonel Arbuthnot see as he returned to his room?

6. What is Hardman's true identity? In what way did he work for Ratchett?

7. Describe Antonio Foscarelli.

8. Why is Mary Debenham not distressed about the murder?

9. What does Mary Debenham think of Poirot's investigation?

10. How does Mary Debenham describe the woman in the scarlet kimono?

Part 2: Chapters 12–15

1. What misconception does Poirot hope to dispel?

2. How does Poirot deal differently with Hildegarde Schmidt than with Mary Debenham?

3. What is unique about the conductor Hildegarde Schmidt met in the hallway?

4. What are the three possibilities regarding the time of the crime?

5. Explain Poirot's theory about the small man with a womanish voice.

6. Who finds the murder weapon? Where is it found, and what does Dr. Constantine say about the weapon?

7. After moving Mrs. Hubbard to a different cabin, how does Poirot continue his investigation?

8. What does Poirot find in Colonel Arbuthnot's bags, and how does the Colonel respond?

9. What gives Poirot pause about searching Count Andrenyi's bags, and how does Andrenyi respond?

10. Where does Poirot find the conductor's uniform, and what does he find in his own luggage?

Part 3: Chapters 1–5

1. What does Poirot reveal about the voice coming from Ratchett's room the night of the murder?

2. How does Poirot feel about Pierre Michel's guilt, considering the evidence?

3. According to M. Bouc and Dr. Constantine, who owns the handkerchief with the "H" sewn into it?

4. How does Poirot feel about M. Bouc's theory that a "Second Murderer" tampered with Ratchett's watch?

5. As Poirot, Bouc, and Dr. Constantine quietly ponder the case, what does the doctor think about?

6. Which minor points strike Poirot as being important and "suggestive"?

7. What is hiding behind the grease spot on Countess Andrenyi's passport, and what implications does this have on the case?

8. Who owns the handkerchief, and how does Poirot discover this person?

9. Why did Princess Dragomiroff lie about knowing Mrs. Armstrong's sister was on the train?

10. How does Poirot propose to proceed with the investigation?

Part 3: Chapters 6–9

1. What does Poirot really want to know from Colonel Arbuthnot? How does Arbuthnot respond?

2. What connection does Mary Debenham have with the Armstrong family?

3. Why does Mary Debenham say she lied to Poirot?

4. How does Poirot discover Antonio Foscarelli's connection to the Armstrong family?

5. What is Masterman's connection to the Armstrong family, and how does he describe Antonio Foscarelli?

6. In Poirot's first conclusion, how does the murderer get on the train?

7. How do M. Bouc and Dr. Constantine react to Poirot's first conclusion?

8. What is the "first and most important" point that Poirot mentions in his second conclusion?

9. What is the symbolic importance of the 12 stab wounds?

10. What is Mrs. Hubbard's true identity?

11. Who is the only innocent passenger once suspected of the murder?

Name _____

Feelings

Directions: Choose a character from the novel, and complete the chart below.

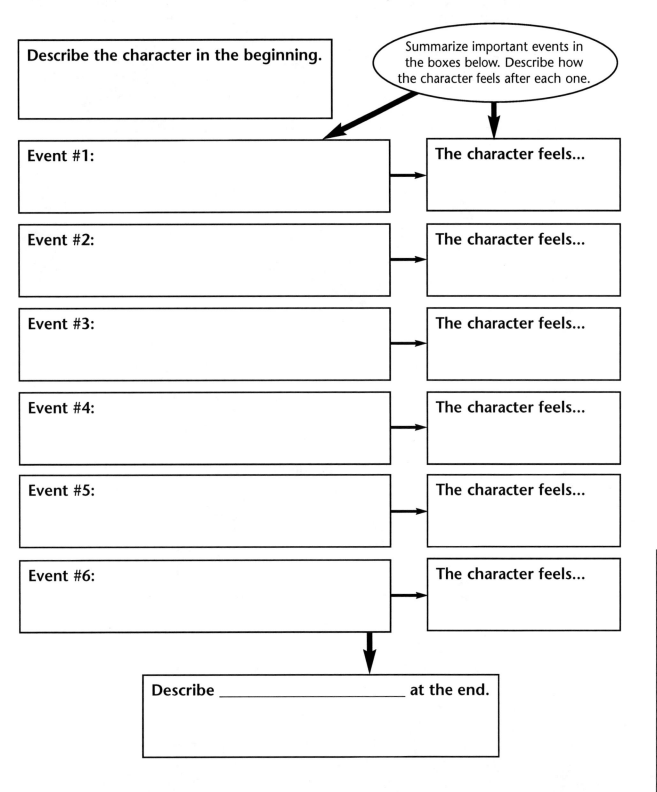

Describe the character in the beginning.

Summarize important events in the boxes below. Describe how the character feels after each one.

Event #1:

The character feels...

Event #2:

The character feels...

Event #3:

The character feels...

Event #4:

The character feels...

Event #5:

The character feels...

Event #6:

The character feels...

Describe _____ at the end.

Cause/Effect

Directions: To plot cause and effect in a story, first list the sequence of events. Then mark causes with a C and effects with an E. Sometimes in a chain of events, one item may be both a cause and an effect. Draw arrows from cause statements to the appropriate effects.

Events in the story	Cause	Effect
1.		
2.		
3.		
4.		
5.		
6.		
7.		
8.		
9.		
10.		

Another way to map cause and effect is to look for an effect and then backtrack to the single or multiple causes.

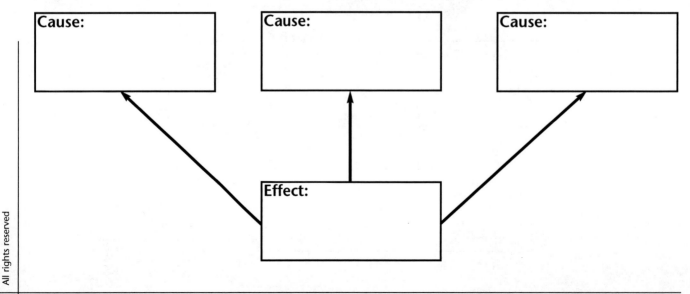

Name _____

Sociogram

Directions: A sociogram shows the relationship between characters in a story. Complete the sociogram below by writing a word to describe the relationships between the characters. Remember, relationships go both ways, so each line requires a descriptive word.

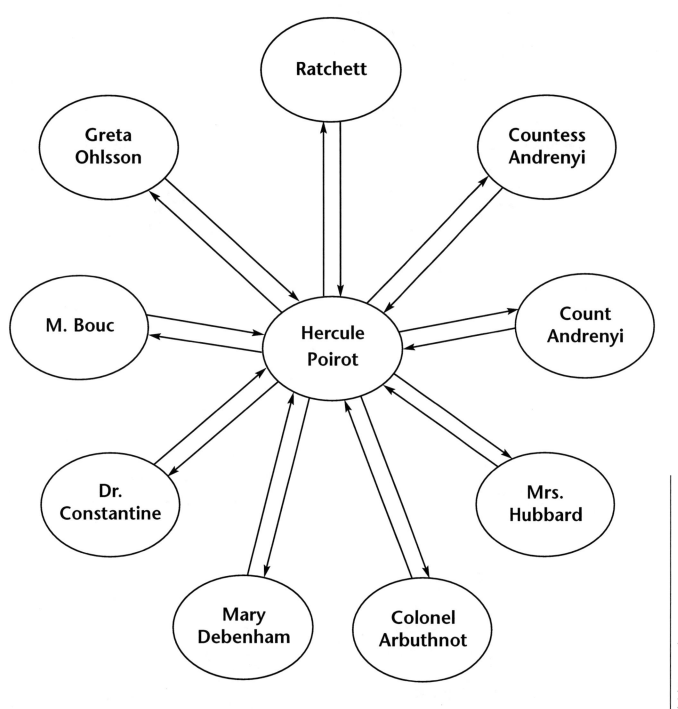

Name _____

Character Web

Directions: Complete the attribute web by filling in information specific to a character in the novel.

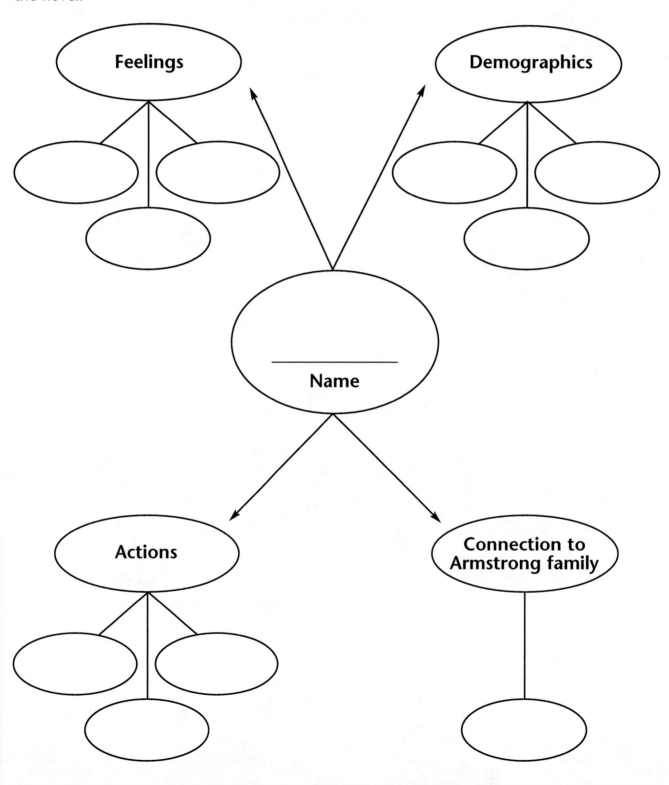

Name _____

Foreshadowing Chart

Foreshadowing is the literary technique of giving clues to coming events in a story.

Directions: What examples of foreshadowing do you recall from the story? If necessary, skim through the chapters to find examples of foreshadowing. List at least four examples below. Explain what clues are given, and then list the coming event that is suggested.

Foreshadowing	Page #	Clues	Coming Event

Name _____

Conflict

The **conflict** of a story is the struggle between two people or two forces. There are four main types of conflict: person vs. person, person vs. nature, person vs. society, and person vs. self.

Directions: In the space provided, list four conflicts a character experiences and justify why you identify it with that particular type of conflict. Then explain how each conflict is resolved in the story.

person vs. person

Conflict	Resolution

person vs. nature

Conflict	Resolution

person vs. society

Conflict	Resolution

person vs. self

Conflict	Resolution

Name _____

Story Map

Directions: Fill in each box below with information about the novel.

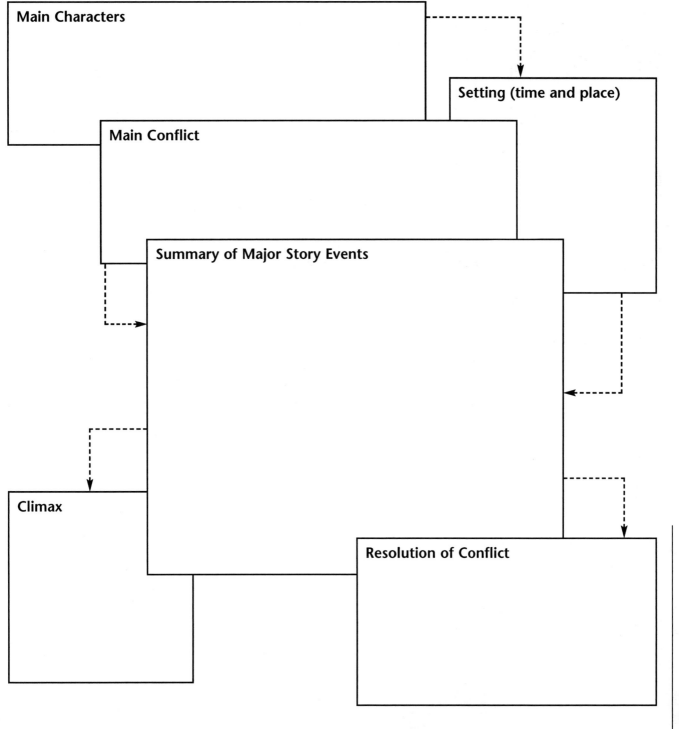

Main Characters

Setting (time and place)

Main Conflict

Summary of Major Story Events

Climax

Resolution of Conflict

Using Dialogue

Directions: Choose some dialogue from the novel. Fill in the chart to evaluate the purpose of the dialogue and whether or not it is effective in moving along the plot.

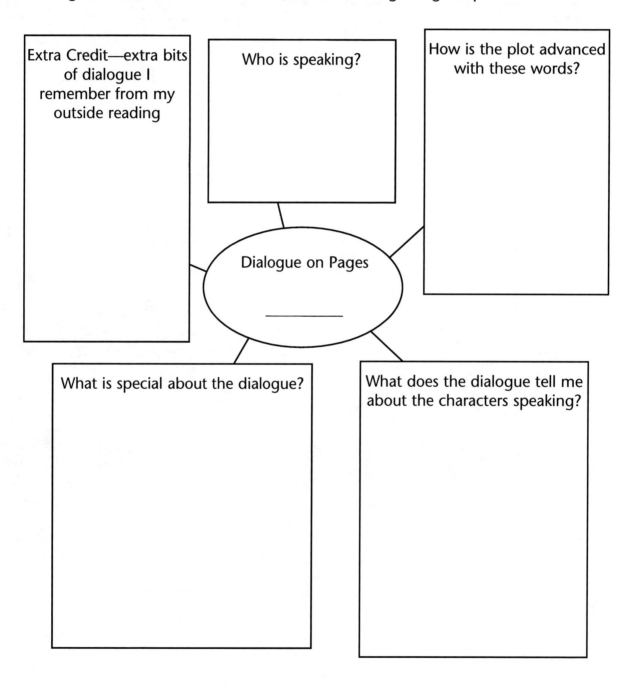

Extra Credit—extra bits of dialogue I remember from my outside reading

Who is speaking?

How is the plot advanced with these words?

Dialogue on Pages

_____

What is special about the dialogue?

What does the dialogue tell me about the characters speaking?

(Main Idea and Details)
A. True/False: Mark each with a *T* for true or an *F* for false.

____ 1. Colonel Arbuthnot suggests that Poirot should visit La Sainte Sophie.

____ 2. Mary Debenham is distraught when she learns a small fire has delayed the train.

____ 3. Hector MacQueen is frustrated because he must share a cabin with Poirot.

____ 4. Poirot tells Ratchett that he is surprised the man only has one enemy.

____ 5. Ratchett threatens Poirot with a pistol when Poirot rejects his money.

(Main Idea and Details)
B. Fill in the Blanks

6. _____ offers _____ 20 thousand dollars to work for him.

7. Colonel Arbuthnot is traveling from his post in _____.

8. Poirot is able to secure a cabin aboard the train when _____ fails to arrive on time.

9. Mrs. Hubbard says she is scared of _____, especially since their two cabins share a _____.

10. A loud _____ and the sound of a _____ awakens Poirot from his sleep.

(Inferences/Predictions)
C. Open-Ended Comprehension: On the lines below, explain why Poirot finds the conversation between Mary Debenham and Colonel Arbuthnot so peculiar.

_____

_____

_____

_____

_____

_____

_____

(Summarize Major Ideas)
A. Short Answer: Write brief answers to each question below.

1. Why is the train so quiet the night of the murder?

   _____

2. Why is Poirot confused by Mary Debenham's demeanor?

   _____

3. What does the *chef de train* conclude about the murder?

   _____

4. How was the murderer able to catch Ratchett by surprise?

   _____

5. What connection did Ratchett have to the Armstrong family?

   _____

(Main Idea and Details)
B. True/False: Mark each with a *T* for true or an *F* for false.

_____ 6. Dr. Constantine is convinced the murderer is left-handed.

_____ 7. Poirot finds two different matches in Ratchett's room.

_____ 8. Poirot believes the threatening letters were written by numerous people.

_____ 9. Hector MacQueen says he enjoyed working for Ratchett.

_____ 10. Ratchett revealed his true identity to MacQueen one week before the murder.

(Making Connections)
C. Open-Ended Comprehension: On the lines below, describe which of the clues found in Ratchett's room you think is the most important and why.

_____

_____

_____

_____

_____

Name _____

(Main Idea and Details)
A. Fill in the Blanks

1. M. Bouc says _____ _____ is respectable and honest, though not too bright.

2. The conductor says he saw a woman wearing a _____ kimono.

3. Masterman admits that he does not care much for _____.

4. Greta Ohlsson shares a cabin with _____ _____.

5. Princess Dragomiroff says her meeting with Hercule Poirot is _____.

(Character Analysis)
B. Identification: Match each character with his/her correct description.

____ 6. Princess Dragomiroff   a. spoke with Colonel Arbuthnot all night

____ 7. Greta Ohlsson   b. found a button in her room

____ 8. Hector MacQueen   c. is Mrs. Armstrong's god-mother

____ 9. Mrs. Hubbard   d. had a toothache the night of the murder

____ 10. Edward Henry Masterman   e. thinks Americans are very practical

(Support Responses)
C. Open-Ended Comprehension: On the lines below, explain your feelings about Princess Dragomiroff's departing statement during her interview with Poirot.

_____

_____

_____

_____

_____

_____

_____

_____

_____

_____

_____

Name _____

(Summarize Major Ideas)
A. Short Answer: Write brief answers to each question below.

1. How does Poirot convince Count Andrenyi to allow him to interrogate the Countess?

   _____

2. What is Colonel Arbuthnot's explanation for not returning to England on the P. & O. boat?

   _____

3. Where was Colonel Arbuthnot the night of the murder?

   _____

4. What is suspicious about the description of the small man with a womanish voice?

   _____

5. Why doesn't the murder distress Mary Debenham?

   _____

(Main Idea and Details)
B. True/False: Mark each with a *T* for true or an *F* for false.

_____ 6. Mary Debenham describes the woman in the scarlet kimono as tall and slim.

_____ 7. Cyrus Hardman is really a detective from Chicago.

_____ 8. Colonel Arbuthnot does not trust the trial by jury system.

_____ 9. Countess Andrenyi was given a sleeping draught the night of the murder.

_____ 10. Ratchett hired Hardman to watch for a small man with a womanish voice.

(Interpret Text)
C. Open-Ended Comprehension: On the lines below, explain Poirot's investigative approach when dealing with Mary Debenham.

_____

_____

_____

_____

_____

(Main Idea and Details)
A. True/False: Mark each with a *T* for true or an *F* for false.

____ 1. Dr. Constantine is suspicious of Mary Debenham because she is so unemotional.

____ 2. Mrs. Hubbard refuses to return to her cabin, so Poirot moves her to a different room.

____ 3. Greta Ohlsson finds a bloody knife in Mrs. Hubbard's sponge-bag.

____ 4. Hildegarde Schmidt always carries the keys to Princess Dragomiroff's luggage.

____ 5. Mary Debenham thinks Poirot is wasting his time by not being direct.

(Character Analysis)
B. Identification: Match each character with his/her correct description.

____ 6. Hildegarde Schmidt   a. asked Greta Ohlsson to lock her door

____ 7. Mrs. Hubbard   b. met a strange conductor in the hallway

____ 8. Cyrus Hardman   c. says the murder weapon is a common dagger

____ 9. Dr. Constantine   d. implores Poirot to show the impossible is possible

____ 10. M. Bouc   e. has liquor hidden in luggage

(Drawing Conclusions)
C. Open-Ended Comprehension: On the lines below, explain why Poirot is not pleased by Dr. Constantine's belief that the bloody knife is the murder weapon.

_____

_____

_____

_____

_____

_____

_____

_____

_____

_____

(Main Idea and Details)
A. Fill in the Blanks

1. Dr. Constantine says that _____ _____ is far too frail to have inflicted the wounds on Ratchett's body.

2. _____ _____ denies owning the handkerchief but admits to being Mrs. Armstrong's sister.

3. Poirot says the murder was initially planned to look like a(n) _____ job.

4. While quietly thinking, Dr. Constantine wishes that the murder had been committed with a _____ instead and dreams of traveling to _____ someday.

5. Poirot finds the _____ _____ on the Countess' _____ highly suspicious.

(Character Analysis)
B. Identification: Match each character with his/her correct description.

____ 6. Hector MacQueen

____ 7. Helena Goldenberg

____ 8. Natalia

____ 9. Princess Dragomiroff

____ 10. Miss Freebody

a. Countess Andrenyi's true identity

b. Princess Dragomiroff's Christian name

c. a governess allegedly working for the Armstrong family

d. owns the mysterious handkerchief

e. notes that Ratchett did not know any foreign languages

(Point of View)
C. Open-Ended Comprehension: On the lines below, explain Poirot's theory about liars.

_____
_____
_____
_____
_____
_____
_____
_____
_____

Name _____

(Main Idea and Details)
A. True/False: Mark each with a *T* for true or an *F* for false.

____ 1. Mary Debenham reveals herself to be Mrs. Armstrong's mother.

____ 2. Dr. Constantine is not pleased with Poirot's first conclusion.

____ 3. Cyrus Hardman threatens to break every bone in Poirot's body.

____ 4. Poirot says the plot could only work if the conductor were involved.

____ 5. Colonel Armstrong saved Masterman's life during the War.

(Main Idea and Details)
B. Fill in the Blanks

6. Susanne, the Armstrong family's French maid, was the daughter of _____
_____.

7. In Poirot's first conclusion, the murderer got on the train in _____.

8. _____ _____ is the only passenger that had nothing to do with
the murder.

9. Poirot says the _____ _____ found in Ratchett's room is of no
consequence.

10. Antonio Foscarelli says that _____ was the "delight" of the Armstrong house.

(Drawing Conclusions)
C. Open-Ended Comprehension: On the lines below, explain why M. Bouc and
Dr. Constantine choose Poirot's second conclusion.

_____
_____
_____
_____
_____
_____
_____
_____
_____
_____

Name _____

(Character Analysis)

A. Identification: Match each character with the BEST description.

____ 1. Pierre Michel

a. believes the murderer is a woman

____ 2. Mrs. Hubbard

b. served as a translator for Ratchett

____ 3. Helena Goldenberg

c. Susanne's father; Wagon Lit employee

____ 4. *chef de train*

d. served as a valet for Ratchett

____ 5. Hercule Poirot

e. wealthy traveler who tried to hire Poirot

____ 6. Mary Debenham

f. tells Ratchett he does not like his face

____ 7. Hector MacQueen

g. Countess Andrenyi's real name

____ 8. Ratchett

h. Daisy Armstrong's governess

____ 9. Edward Henry Masterman

i. Mrs. Armstrong's god-mother

____ 10. Princess Dragomiroff

j. constantly mentions her daughter; finds bloody knife

B. Multiple Choice: Choose the BEST answer to each of the following.

(Setting)

____ 11. What is the name of the main sleeping car on the Orient Express?

(a) Syria-Paris car

(b) Athens-Paris car

(c) Tokatlian-Calais car

(d) Stamboul-Calais car

(Main Idea and Details)

____ 12. What relationship does Hector MacQueen have with the Armstrong family?

(a) He served as the Armstrong family's chauffeur.

(b) His father was a detective in the Armstrong case.

(c) He served as Colonel Armstrong's military servant.

(d) His father was the district attorney in charge of the Armstrong case.

(Main Idea and Details)

____ 13. Antonio Foscarelli spent the night of the murder in a shared cabin with

    (a) Cyrus Hardman

    (b) Dr. Constantine

    (c) Masterman

    (d) Pierre Michel

(Main Idea and Details)

____ 14. Countess Andrenyi's real name is Helena

    (a) Arden

    (b) Armstrong

    (c) Goldenberg

    (d) Harris

(Main Idea and Details)

____ 15. What name does Poirot discover on the burnt scrap of letter?

    (a) Cassetti

    (b) Colonel Armstrong

    (c) Daisy Armstrong

    (d) Linda Arden

(Main Idea and Details)

____ 16. The mysterious handkerchief belongs to

    (a) Countess Andrenyi

    (b) Hildegarde Schmidt

    (c) Linda Arden

    (d) Princess Dragomiroff

(Making Connections)

____ 17. Each wound on Ratchett's body is different because

    (a) there were two murderers

    (b) each passenger stabbed him once

    (c) it was too dark for the murderer to see

    (d) the murderer changed hands during the murder

(Main Idea and Details)

____ 18. What excuse does Mary Debenham give for lying about being Daisy Armstrong's governess?

   (a) She is worried about retaliation.

   (b) She is worried about her reputation.

   (c) She is trying to forget her painful past.

   (d) She does not want to get involved with the police.

(Drawing Conclusions)

____ 19. Why does Poirot believe someone drugged Ratchett the night of the murder?

   (a) Ratchett had a fully-loaded gun under his pillow.

   (b) Ratchett never needed a sleeping draught before.

   (c) Poirot found a sleeping draught in Ratchett's cabin.

   (d) Poirot did not hear any noises in Ratchett's cabin that night.

(Point of View)

____ 20. M. Bouc's prejudices lead him to believe the murderer is a(n)

   (a) American

   (b) gangster

   (c) Italian

   (d) woman

(Main Idea and Details)

C. Fill in the Blanks

21. Mrs. Hubbard finds a _____ _____ in her cabin and refuses to sleep there another night.

22. _____ says he could not sleep the night of the murder because he had a toothache.

23. While at the Tokatlian Hotel, _____ receives a telegram recalling him to _____.

24. Poirot finds the _____ _____ hidden in his own luggage.

25. The person in Ratchett's cabin speaks _____, sending the conductor away.

26. Count Andrenyi is a wealthy diplomat from _____.

27. _____ _____ enjoys discussing business methods and life in America.

28. Hildegarde Schmidt met a _____ in the hallway that she did not recognize.

29. The label on Countess Andrenyi's suitcase is _____, arousing Poirot's suspicion.

30. Poirot is convinced that the _____ found on Ratchett's body is a ruse, as well as the open _____.

D. Open-Ended Short Answer: Briefly respond to each of the following.

(Interpret Text)
(a) Explain how Poirot connected Ratchett to the Armstrong kidnapping case.

_____

_____

(Summarize Major Ideas)
(b) Explain Poirot's first conclusion about the crime.

_____

_____

(Character Analysis)
(c) Explain Linda Arden's (Mrs. Hubbard's) defense and justification of Ratchett's murder.

_____

_____

(Locate Information)
(d) Explain the ways in which Ratchett attempted to protect himself from his fate.

_____

_____

E. Essay: On a separate sheet of paper, respond to one of the following in a well-developed essay. Cite specific evidence from the novel to support your answer.

(Character Analysis)
(a) Examine the role M. Bouc and Dr. Constantine each play in Poirot's investigation. Describe what skills and credentials each brings to the investigation, and explain how each aids Poirot in discovering the truth about the crime.

(Summarize Major Ideas)
(b) Explain how Ratchett's murder was planned, carried out, and concealed.

(Character Analysis)
(c) Describe Hercule Poirot. Examine his deductive methods, and explain the major breakthroughs he made in discovering the truth about Ratchett's murder.

Answer Key

Activity #1: Dedication: To M.E.L.M. Arpachiya, 1933; Title: *Murder on the Orient Express*; Cover Illustration: a dining car on a train; Teasers on the cover: "What more...can a mystery addict desire?"—*The New York Times* (back cover); Friends' recommendations: Answers will vary; Reviewers' recommendations/awards won: same quote as listed for teasers; Predictions will vary.

Activity #2: Answers will vary.

Activity #3: Sentences will vary.

Activity #4: 1. c 2. d 3. b 4. b 5. d 6. c 7. d 8. a 9. d 10. b 11. b 12. a

Activity #5: Answers will vary. Suggestion: Word—pacify; Definition—to appease someone for the sake of creating peace; Synonym—soothe, calm, mollify; Antonym—antagonize, upset, annoy; Part of Speech—verb; Pronunciation—pa-sə -fi; Sentence—In order to *pacify* the angry mob, the senator agreed to step down from office.

Activity #6: Associations will vary. Suggestion: Word—animus; Character: Colonel Arbuthnot; Explanation—As Poirot asked more questions about his relationship with Mary Debenham, Colonel Arbuthnot expressed obvious *animus* toward the detective.

Activity #7: 1. drinker/teetotaler 2. validating/corroborating 3. inheritance/bequest 4. valise/portmanteau 5. solemn/coquettish 6. slenderness/rotundity 7. critically/reprovingly 8. poise/*sang-froid* 9. resisted/acquiesced 10. defiant/truculent 11. imprinted/embossed 12. unapologetic/rueful; Antonyms—1, 5, 6, 9, 12

Activity #8: Descriptions will vary.

Activity #9: Crossword puzzles will vary.

Study Guide
Part 1: Chapters 1–4: 1. He judges her as a young woman with "poise and efficiency" who can "take care of herself with perfect ease" (p. 9). 2. She becomes fraught with anxiety and is worried about missing the connecting train. She is so worried that her lips tremble. 3. Although Ratchett is smiling and has the "bland aspect of a philanthropist" (p. 18), Poirot sees a "strange malevolence" in the man's eyes. Ratchett strikes him as wild and savage, a cruel human being hiding behind the mask of a wealthy traveler. 4. Bouc mentions how curious it is that so many people from such different backgrounds happen to be on the remote train at the exact same time. He finds it incredible that after being together in such tight quarters, they will part ways and never see each other again. Poirot wonders if some specific reason has brought them here and mentions murder as a possible link. 5. He says she is Russian and that her husband invested all their money before the Russian Revolution. He calls her "a cosmopolitan" and "a personality." 6. Ratchett has an enemy, and he thinks that enemy will try to kill him. He offers Poirot "big money" to protect him. Poirot turns down the offer, saying he doesn't like Ratchett's face. 7. She is "dead scared" of Ratchett and tells Poirot that there is something wrong with him. She says Ratchett tried to open her door, and she insists that something terrible will happen. 8. Poirot sees a conductor rush down the hall and knock on Ratchett's door. A voice calls out in French, telling the conductor he is not needed.

Part 1: Chapters 5–8: 1. Mrs. Hubbard is terrified and says a man was in her room. The conductor assured her there was not, but she insists it is true and "will not listen to reason" (p. 43). 2. It is stuck in the snow; She is not upset or anxious like she was when the last train ran late. Though she is still demanding and annoyed, she is quite calm and understanding about the delay compared to her previous reaction. 3. It occurred at about one o'clock in the morning, and the window was left open, though likely as a ruse; There are no footsteps in the snow, and there are about a dozen stab wounds on the body. 4. Based on the stab wounds, he is adamant that the murderer is a woman, even though the evidence does not specifically prove this. 5. He was Ratchett's secretary and acted as a courier and translator. 6. The letters were written by more than one person, each person writing one letter of each word. 7. The wounds on Ratchett's body are different sizes and seem to have been inflicted by both a left and right hand with varying strengths. It seems nearly impossible that the wounds were inflicted by only one person, yet the possibility of multiple murderers who stabbed Ratchett at different times sounds absurd to Poirot. 8. After investigating the scrap of letter left in Ratchett's room, Poirot finds that Ratchett was involved with the kidnapping of Daisy Armstrong, and he is able to deduce that Ratchett has been on the run ever since escaping justice in America; Cassetti 9. Daisy Armstrong was kidnapped, held for ransom, and then killed. Mrs. Armstrong was pregnant with another child and died after giving birth. Colonel Armstrong committed suicide. A French maid, after being falsely accused of being involved with the kidnapping, also killed herself. 10. He will speak to each passenger one by one, asking questions and gathering information about their pasts and their activities on the night of the murder.

Part 2: Chapters 1–6: 1. as a "respectable and honest" man that has been a Wagon Lit conductor for over 15 years; He is not overly smart but is a reliable employee. 2. His father was the district attorney in charge of the Armstrong kidnapping case; He feels Cassetti deserves what he got. 3. He was in his cabin speaking to Colonel Arbuthnot for most of the night, and then he went to bed. He saw a woman in a scarlet kimono walk by his door. 4. Masterman was Ratchett's valet, but he only worked for Ratchett for a matter of months; Masterman spent the evening in his cabin with the Italian passenger, Antonio Foscarelli. 5. Mrs. Hubbard vehemently insists that the murderer was in her cabin that night, and while she never actually saw the murderer, she sensed someone was in her room and rang for the conductor. 6. She had him relock the communicating door between her cabin and Ratchett's cabin, as well as block the door with a suitcase. 7. Greta Ohlsson, who stopped by to ask for some medicine 8. Ratchett's room; He made a rude joke at her expense, then returned to reading his book as she left. 9. He thinks the murderer is Antonio Foscarelli because he is Italian, and Bouc believes that Italians use knives to kill people; Poirot doubts Bouc's rash theory and points out that Foscarelli has an alibi. 10. Princess Dragomiroff was Mrs. Armstrong's god-mother and good friends with Linda Arden, Mrs. Armstrong's mother. She tells Poirot that Linda Arden is alive, as well as a second, younger daughter. The younger daughter married an Englishman and moved to England.

Part 2: Chapters 7–11: 1. He takes an authoritative tone and says it is unnecessary. He says there is nothing she can tell Poirot but agrees when Poirot kindly says it will be a simple formality. 2. She was sleeping in her cabin most of the night and heard nothing, due to a sleeping draught. 3. He is on leave from his post in India, and though he sent most of his belongings by boat, he decided to take a train so he may sightsee and visit some old friends. 4. He did not see her, but he knows that she passed by because he sensed "a rustle and a sort of smell of scent" (p. 157). 5. The door beyond his opened, a man looked out in a furtive manner, and then the door closed quickly. It was a small event but struck the Colonel "as a bit odd" (p. 160). 6. He is a private detective in New York City; Ratchett hired Hardman to watch for suspicious characters, specifically a small man with a womanish voice. 7. He walks with "a swift, cat-like tread" and has "a typical Italian face, sunny-looking and swarthy" (p. 173). He likes to talk about America and business tactics, and Poirot has a difficult time keeping Foscarelli on track. 8. While death is "an unpleasant thing," she says "people die every day" (p. 180) and "hysterics" will not prove that she is sensitive to the issue. 9. She does not like Poirot's methods, calling them "a waste of time" (p. 181). His methods of discussing feelings, opinions, and emotions bothers her, and she does not see what her feelings about the victim have to do with the murder. 10. tall, thin, and wearing a cap; The kimono was embroidered with dragons. She did not see the woman's face or hair color.

Part 2: Chapters 12–15: 1. He hopes to dispel the idea that the murder was "an unpremeditated and sudden crime" (p. 188). Both M. Bouc and Dr. Constantine are convinced that the murderer is not a calm thinker but a rash, hot-tempered killer. This misconception is hindering Bouc's and Dr. Constantine's ability to deduce effectively. 2. While Poirot prodded Mary Debenham, hoping she might show some emotion, he is very kind and patient with Hildegarde Schmidt. In this way, he sets her at ease so she might open up. 3. She had never seen the conductor before, and he was certainly not the one who was on duty answering bells. 4. (1) The murder was committed at quarter past one, as indicated by the suspicious broken watch. (2) The watch is a decoy, and the murder was committed before the indicated time on the watch. (3) The watch is a decoy, and the murder was committed after the indicated time on the watch. 5. Because no one on the train fits the description, he admits it is possible this person is actually a woman disguised as a man, which would explain the man's stature and voice. 6. Mrs. Hubbard finds the bloody knife in her sponge-bag; Dr. Constantine confirms it is the same weapon that inflicted the wounds on Ratchett's body. 7. He begins to search each passenger's luggage, starting with Mrs. Hubbard's bags, where he finds nothing of consequence. 8. the same kind of pipe cleaner found in Ratchett's room; Colonel Arbuthnot admits that he uses that type of pipe cleaner as often as possible. 9. As a diplomat, Count Andrenyi is exempt from the investigation, but when Poirot approaches him about the search, Count Andrenyi is more than happy to comply. 10. in Hildegarde Schmidt's luggage; He finds the scarlet kimono in his own luggage, which indicates that the murderer is playing games with him.

Part 3: Chapters 1–5: 1. Poirot says that since Ratchett could not speak French, the person that spoke to the conductor could not have been Ratchett. The murderer, or perhaps someone who stumbled upon the body but did not want to open the door, was the person that spoke. 2. In his notes, Poirot states that he believes the use of a conductor's uniform by the murderer was meant to cast guilt upon the conductor on duty, which makes Pierre Michel appear innocent. 3. M. Bouc believes that Mary Debenham owns the handkerchief because "there is already some suspicion attaching to her" (p. 248) and she may go by a middle name that begins with "H." Dr. Constantine is convinced that Mrs. Hubbard owns the handkerchief because the handkerchief is expensive and Americans "do not care what they pay" (p. 248). They both eliminate Hildegarde Schmidt. 4. Poirot does not believe this theory and questions it by saying sarcastically, "she stabbed him in the dark, not realizing that he was dead already, but somehow deduced that he had a watch in his pyjama pocket, took it out" (p. 251) and reset the time in the dark. 5. He starts to wonder if Poirot is a "genius" or a "crank" and believes the case to be "impossible." He thinks that the case is confusing no matter what evidence the passengers offer. He wishes the wounds were from a gun instead and ponders a trip to America. He then thinks about a woman named Zia, with whom he is having an adulterous relationship. 6. the position of Mrs. Hubbard's sponge-bag, the name of Mrs. Armstrong's mother, Hardman's detective methods, MacQueen's suggestion that Ratchett destroyed the letter, Princess Dragomiroff's Christian name, and the grease spot on Countess Andrenyi's passport 7. the first letter in Countess Andrenyi's first name; Her real name is Helena Goldenberg. She is the sister of Mrs. Armstrong and Linda Arden's daughter, making her the passenger with the closest connection to the Armstrong family. 8. Poirot first believes that Helena, Countess Andrenyi, owns the handkerchief, but she insists she does not. Then Princess Dragomiroff enters the dining car and says that she owns the handkerchief, and that the "H" is from her Christian name. 9. She says she lied about knowing Helena because she is loyal to Linda Arden. She thinks strict justice has been done, and she would lie about it again if given the chance. 10. He sees now that many of the passengers are lying, and he proposes to speak to them again and guess which parts of their stories are false. He believes if he can reveal their lies, they will admit them and reveal the truth.

Part 3: Chapters 6–9: 1. Even though he first asks about the pipe cleaner, Poirot really wants to know what Arbuthnot and Mary Debenham discussed during their hushed, secret conversation, specifically what Mary meant when she said "*Not now. When it's all over. When it's behind us!*" (p. 285); Colonel Arbuthnot says his "lips are sealed" and refuses to "give away a lady's secret" (p. 285). Later, when Poirot pressures Mary Debenham to reveal her secret, Colonel Arbuthnot threatens to break every bone in Poirot's body. 2. Poirot guesses that she was Daisy Armstrong's governess. Colonel Arbuthnot denies this, but Mary later admits it is true. 3. She has a reputation to maintain as a governess, and no one will hire her if they hear she was on the same train as Ratchett when he died, considering he destroyed the family she used to work for. The publicity would ruin her. 4. Poirot says he knows the truth about him and would like Antonio Foscarelli to admit he lied. The Italian says Poirot sounds just like the police. When Poirot asks if he has had trouble with the New York police, Foscarelli says, "They could not prove a thing against me" (p. 294). Realizing his mistake, Foscarelli then admits he was the Armstrong family's chauffeur and that he cared for little Daisy Armstrong very much. 5. He served as Colonel Armstrong's military servant, and they became quite close. He apologizes to Poirot for hiding this but also says he hopes Poirot does not suspect "Tonio" of any wrongdoing. He describes Antonio Foscarelli as "a very gentle creature" who "wouldn't hurt a fly" (pp. 297–298). 6. He enters the train through the door Colonel Arbuthnot and MacQueen accidentally left open after they descended to the platform for a short walk in Vincovci. 7. Bouc questions some elements of the story but resigns himself to the idea that it may be possible. Dr. Constantine, on the other hand, is incredulous and vehemently denies this explanation, insisting that it does not fit all the known facts. 8. Bouc noticed that the train, usually empty this time of year, is crowded with diverse and unique characters from different nationalities and classes. Such a collection at such a time seems improbable, and Poirot began to wonder if there were connections between the passengers. 9. There are 12 stab wounds, one for each passenger on the train, and the 12 people form a "jury" seeking personal vengeance against Ratchett. 10. She is really the actress Linda Arden, Mrs. Armstrong's mother. 11. Countess Andrenyi, to whom Count Andrenyi administered a sleeping draught so she would not become a part of the crime; He took her place.

Note: Responses to Activities #10–#17 will vary. Suggested answers have been given where applicable.

Activity #10: Suggestions for Mrs. Hubbard/Linda Arden: In the beginning: She is extremely talkative; Event #1: She tells other passengers about her daughter as the trip begins—excited; Event #2: She discusses Ratchett with Poirot—troubled; Event #3: She senses someone in her room—terrified; Event #4: Poirot moves her to a different cabin—relieved; Event #5: She listens to Poirot's first conclusion—placid and accepting; Event #6: Poirot reveals her to be Linda Arden—calm and complimentary, yet steadfast in her belief that justice has been served; At the end: satisfied and ready to accept blame

Activity #11: Answers will vary.

Activity #12: Suggestion: Hercule Poirot to Greta Ohlsson: patient; Greta Ohlsson to Hercule Poirot: fretful; Hercule Poirot to Colonel Arbuthnot: respectful then pushy; Colonel Arbuthnot to Hercule Poirot: compliant then angry

Activity #13: Suggestion for Antonio Foscarelli: Feelings—excited, disturbed, sorrowful; Demographics—Italian, salesman, traveler; Actions—friendly, unfocused, stabbed Ratchett once; Connection to Armstrong family—chauffeur

Activity #14: Suggestion: Foreshadowing—conspiracy; Page #—26; Clues—Bouc and Poirot notice that the train is filled with a diverse group of people, and Poirot wonders if there is some sinister reason for everyone to be in the same place; Coming Event—Death will bring these people together.

Activity #15: Suggestion: person vs. person: Conflict—Poirot wants to know the meaning of Mary Debenham and Colonel Arbuthnot's conversation. They refuse to speak, and Arbuthnot becomes confrontational. Resolution—Poirot is able to guess that Mary Debenham was Daisy Armstrong's governess and that the two know each other from their past with the Armstrong family; person vs. nature: Conflict—The train is stuck in the snow, and Poirot cannot elicit outside help to verify the personal histories of certain passengers. Resolution—Poirot is forced to guess, make assumptions, and follow his instincts; person vs. society: Conflict—Many of the passengers belong to certain class levels, and their servants remain loyal, creating problems with the reliability of eyewitness details. Resolution—By guessing at which parts of stories are lies, Poirot is able to make people confess to lies and admit the truth; person vs. self: Conflict—When asked to quietly think of the case, M. Bouc and Dr. Constantine attempt to think of the details but quickly drift to other topics and come up with no solutions. Resolution—While their deductive methods failed them, Poirot is able to use them to test his ideas or flush out what details they think are important and compare them to his own thoughts.

Activity #16: Main Characters: Hercule Poirot, M. Bouc, Dr. Constantine, Pierre Michel, Ratchett, Mary Debenham, Colonel Arbuthnot, Hector MacQueen, Antonio Foscarelli, Edward Henry Masterman, Cyrus Hardman, Princess Dragomiroff, Greta Ohlsson, Mrs. Hubbard, Hildegarde Schmidt, Count and Countess Andrenyi; Setting: the passenger cars of the Orient Express, stuck in the snow in the Yugoslavian mountains; Main Conflict: Ratchett has been murdered in his cabin, and Poirot must determine which of the passengers committed the crime; Summary of Major Story Events: Poirot is traveling on the Orient Express. One of the passengers, Ratchett, approaches Poirot with a job offer—protect him from the person trying to kill him. Poirot refuses, and Ratchett is murdered in his cabin. The train is stuck in the snow, and Poirot begins his investigation into the murder. He discovers that Ratchett was really Cassetti, an evil man that kidnapped and killed Daisy Armstrong, a little American girl. Poirot interviews each of the passengers, trying to determine details about their pasts and what they know of Ratchett/Cassetti; Climax: Each passenger is eventually revealed to be connected to the Armstrong family, and Poirot determines that each of them took part in the murder; Resolution of Conflict: No one is held responsible for Ratchett's murder, as everyone on the train believes that justice was served.

Activity #17: Answers will vary.

Quiz #1: A. 1. F 2. T 3. F 4. T 5. F **B.** 6. Ratchett; Poirot 7. India 8. Mr. Harris 9. Ratchett; door 10. groan or cry; bell **C.** Answers will vary. Refer to the scoring rubric on page 42 of this guide.

Quiz #2: A. 1. It stopped moving because of the snow blocking the tracks. 2. She was upset when the train stopped moving before, but now she is abnormally calm. 3. He is convinced the murderer is a woman. 4. Ratchett was drugged and asleep when the murderer approached. 5. He kidnapped and killed Daisy Armstrong. **B.** 6. F 7. T 8. T 9. F 10. F **C.** Answers will vary. Refer to the scoring rubric on page 42 of this guide.

Quiz #3: A. 1. Pierre Michel 2. scarlet 3. Americans 4. Mary Debenham 5. Destiny **B.** 6. c 7. e 8. a 9. b 10. d **C.** Answers will vary. Refer to the scoring rubric on page 42 of this guide.

Quiz #4: A. 1. He politely explains it is a mere formality and necessary for his report. 2. He sent his luggage via boat and returned by train for his own personal reasons. He does not fully explain these reasons but does state that he has toured numerous cities along the way. 3. talking with Hector MacQueen in MacQueen's cabin 4. The description does not apply to anyone on the train. 5. She says that people die every day and even though it is an unpleasant thing, becoming hysterical will not benefit her at all. **B.** 6. T 7. F 8. F 9. T 10. T **C.** Answers will vary. Refer to the scoring rubric on page 42 of this guide.

Quiz #5: A. 1. F 2. T 3. F 4. T 5. T **B.** 6. b 7. a 8. e 9. c 10. d **C.** Answers will vary. Refer to the scoring rubric on page 42 of this guide.

Quiz #6: A. 1. Princess Dragomiroff 2. Countess Andrenyi or Helena Goldenberg 3. outside 4. gun; America 5. grease spot; passport **B.** 6. e 7. a 8. b 9. d 10. c **C.** Answers will vary. Refer to the scoring rubric on page 42 of this guide.

Quiz #7: A. 1. F 2. T 3. F 4. T 5. F **B.** 6. Pierre Michel 7. Vincovci 8. Countess Andrenyi 9. pipe cleaner 10. Daisy **C.** Answers will vary. Refer to the scoring rubric on page 42 of this guide.

Novel Test: A. 1. c 2. j 3. g 4. a 5. f 6. h 7. b 8. e 9. d 10. i **B.** 11. d 12. d 13. c 14. c 15. c 16. d 17. b 18. b 19. a 20. c **C.** 21. bloody knife 22. Masterman 23. Poirot; London 24. scarlet kimono 25. French 26. Hungary 27. Antonio Foscarelli 28. conductor 29. wet or damp 30. watch; window **D.–E.** Answers will vary. Refer to the scoring rubric on page 42 of this guide.

Linking Novel Units® Student Packets to National and State Reading Assessments

During the past several years, an increasing number of students have faced some form of state-mandated competency testing in reading. Many states now administer state-developed assessments to measure the skills and knowledge emphasized in their particular reading curriculum. This Novel Units® guide includes open-ended comprehension questions that correlate with state-mandated reading assessments. The rubric below provides important information for evaluating responses to open-ended comprehension questions. Teachers may also use scoring rubrics provided for their own state's competency test.

Scoring Rubric for Open-Ended Items

3-Exemplary	Thorough, complete ideas/information Clear organization throughout Logical reasoning/conclusions Thorough understanding of reading task Accurate, complete response
2-Sufficient	Many relevant ideas/pieces of information Clear organization throughout most of response Minor problems in logical reasoning/conclusions General understanding of reading task Generally accurate and complete response
1-Partially Sufficient	Minimally relevant ideas/information Obvious gaps in organization Obvious problems in logical reasoning/conclusions Minimal understanding of reading task Inaccuracies/incomplete response
0-Insufficient	Irrelevant ideas/information No coherent organization Major problems in logical reasoning/conclusions Little or no understanding of reading task Generally inaccurate/incomplete response

Notes

Notes